Acoustic Masterclass

KENNY SULTAN
Guitar Blues

Project Manager: Aaron Stang
Transcription Editors: Louis Martinez and Colgan Bryan
Art Layout and Design: Jorge Paredes

© 2004 WARNER BROS. PUBLICATIONS
All Rights Reserved

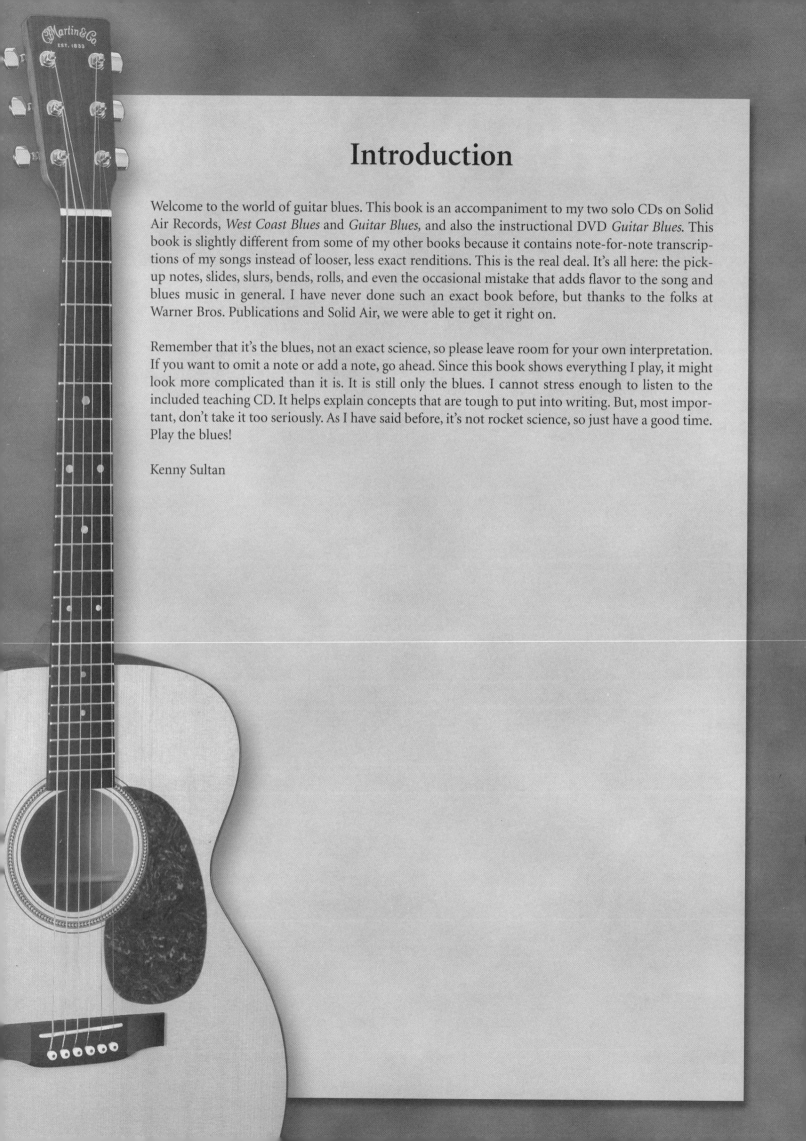

Introduction

Welcome to the world of guitar blues. This book is an accompaniment to my two solo CDs on Solid Air Records, *West Coast Blues* and *Guitar Blues,* and also the instructional DVD *Guitar Blues.* This book is slightly different from some of my other books because it contains note-for-note transcriptions of my songs instead of looser, less exact renditions. This is the real deal. It's all here: the pick-up notes, slides, slurs, bends, rolls, and even the occasional mistake that adds flavor to the song and blues music in general. I have never done such an exact book before, but thanks to the folks at Warner Bros. Publications and Solid Air, we were able to get it right on.

Remember that it's the blues, not an exact science, so please leave room for your own interpretation. If you want to omit a note or add a note, go ahead. Since this book shows everything I play, it might look more complicated than it is. It is still only the blues. I cannot stress enough to listen to the included teaching CD. It helps explain concepts that are tough to put into writing. But, most important, don't take it too seriously. As I have said before, it's not rocket science, so just have a good time. Play the blues!

Kenny Sultan

Contents

The Compositions

Cascade Rag

The first song, "Cascade Rag," is a ragtime blues piece. It starts off on the B part, or bridge, which is a little unusual, but then it evolves into the typical V-I-V-I-V-I turnaround pattern. I use several different positions for the chords to keep it interesting. Once you master it, try to add a few of them yourself.

There are a few tricky right-hand rolls, so be sure to listen to the teaching CD to get the proper feel. Start slowly with this tune and then work it up to speed. Good luck!

Funky Butt

This song is a little different from most of the things I play in the key of E in that it is a rag, not a blues. Usually I play ragtime in C or G. Watch out for the C♯9 and F♯ chords. Making these chords sound clean is hard if you are not used to playing them. Just keep at it and they will come around. I explain on the CD how to cheat a bit, so heads up on that.

You'll find some difficult hammer-ons in measures 41–43 and 48–49. First try picking them without the hammers to get the timing, and then add the hammers when you feel comfortable.

Honky Tonk

This song also deviates a little from my tendencies in that it is a 12-bar blues in the key of C (don't worry—lots of E blues coming up). The hardest parts for me are the numerous runs and double-bassing (two bass notes per beat. There is definitely a Big Bill Broonzy thing going on here. Play this song slowly and with feeling, just as you would a standard blues. Check the CD to learn the tricks.

Ream 'Em and Weep

I play this song down a half step to make it sound funky—as Lightnin' Hopkins used to do. If you have an extra guitar to put in this tuning, it's kind of fun. The bends become bigger as the strings become looser in this tuning (or maybe you get looser as the as the night wears on). Play it like you mean it!

Lightnin' Strikes

This is a typical call-and-response kind of blues in the key of E. I bounce between rhythm and lead or fills. I use a lot of double-stops (two notes at once) to give it some extra kick. Also, by resting your right hand on the bass strings, you create a more percussive quality by muting the low E and A strings a bit. Check out the CD to hear what I'm talking about.

If the Shoe Fits

"If the Shoe Fits" has a bit of a jazzy feel to it because of the slides and 9th chords. I make partial 9ths instead of complete 9ths in this song, which helps smooth out the slides. Before you start the slide, be sure to get a nice big sound going to help carry the tone throughout the measure.

The Sick Boogie

"The Sick Boogie" is just that: a boogie in the key of A that got out of control. We were messing around in the studio, playing fast and proud, and they happened to be running tape. I use finger-style technique here, but it could almost be done with a flatpick. It is basically similar in nature to our other blues—but hyper-speed. I alternate between my right-hand thumb and index finger for the lead parts. This song is way more feel than technique, so let it fly!

Slippin' and Drippin'

"Slippin' and Drippin'" is played in the position of E tuned down a half step, which again makes it sound very funky, but you don't need to tune down to have a real blues on your hands. Play it as slowly as you can and still keep a rhythm going. You will notice some double-bassing and some very cool bends. I explain these techniques on the teaching CD, so be sure to use it as a guide. Have fun.

West Coast Blues

"West Coast Blues" is what I play and improvise on when I'm just hanging out at my house, and it is my standard sound-check song at gigs. It pretty much has it all going for a mid-paced blues. I modeled it after an Eddie "Cleanhead" Vincent lick I heard as a kid. Originally it was played on saxophone, but I tailored it for guitar. It's trickier than it sounds. Watch out for the 9th chords and the timing throughout. Check out the CD of the same name or the teaching CD included with this book.

Suspicious Strut

"Suspicious Strut" is the first true rag in this book and arguably the hardest song, which is why I saved it for last. I capo on the 2nd fret, which makes it easier to handle and gives it a higher-pitched ragtime feel. You get it all here: alternating bass, moving bass, lead lines on the treble strings, counterpoint, and a big headache for about a week trying to learn the first few measures. Don't worry though: it gets easier as you get into it. Listen to the CD, and good luck!

Cascade Rag

By KENNY SULTAN

Moderately fast ragtime, in 2 ♩ = 120

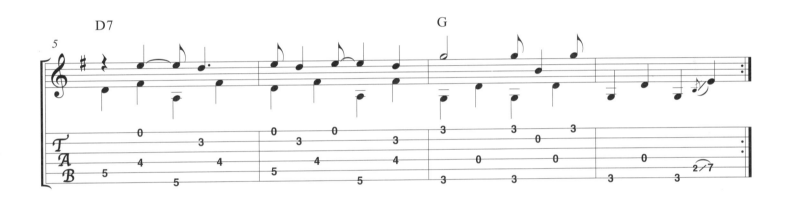

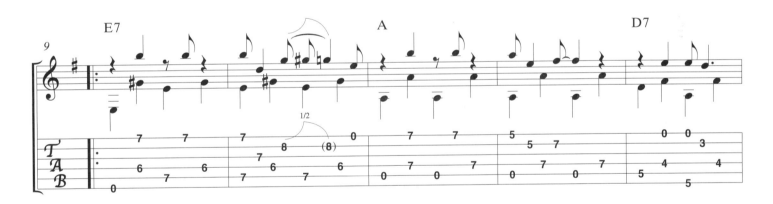

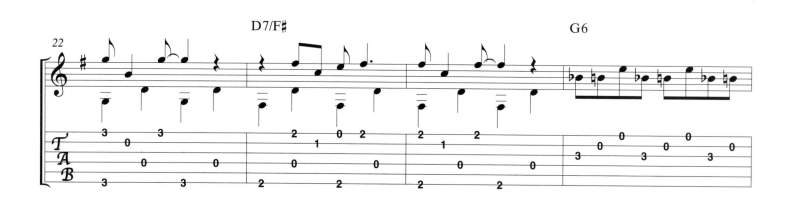

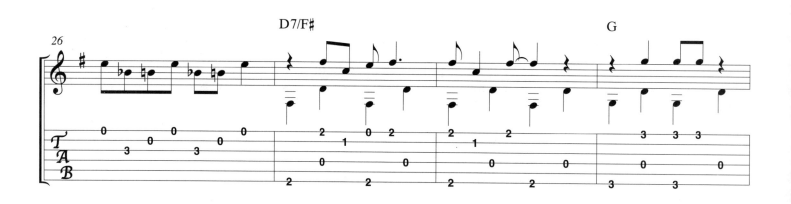

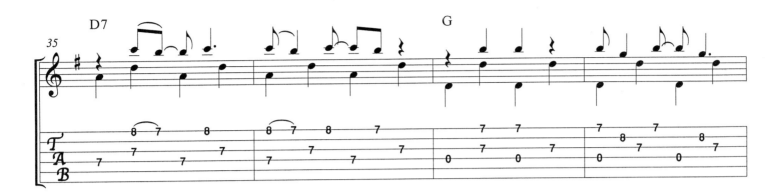

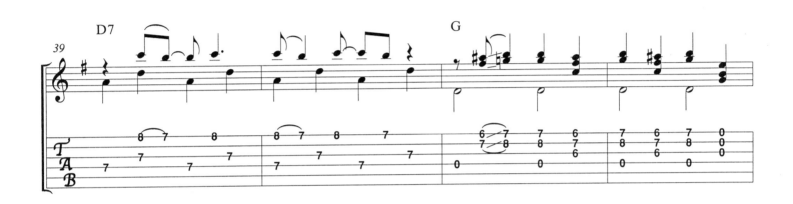

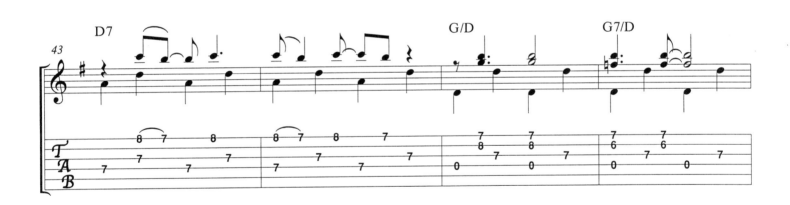

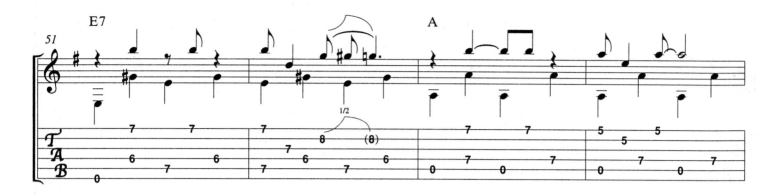

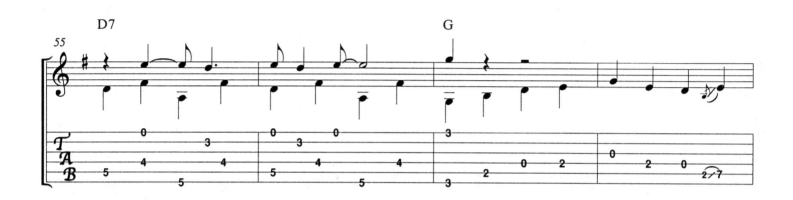

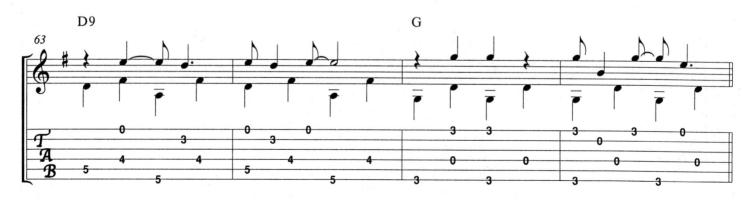

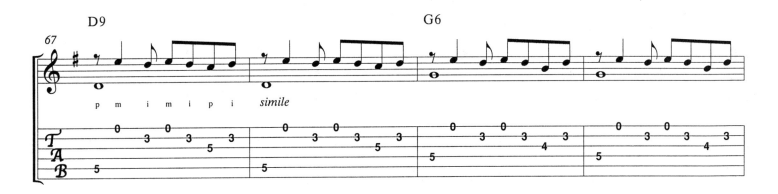

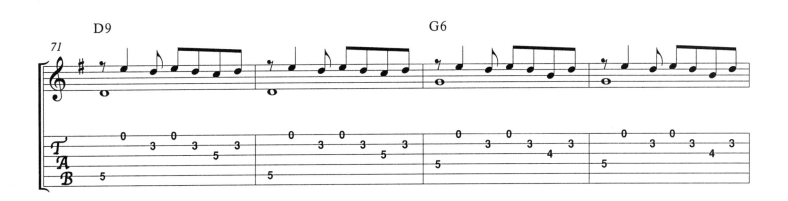

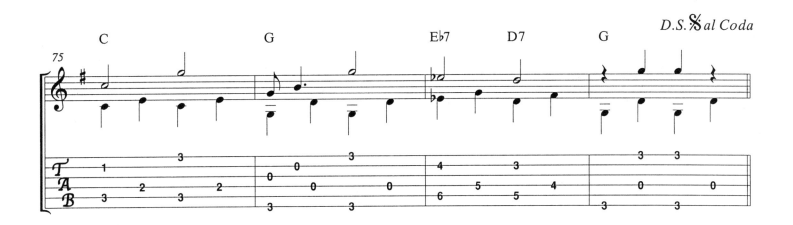

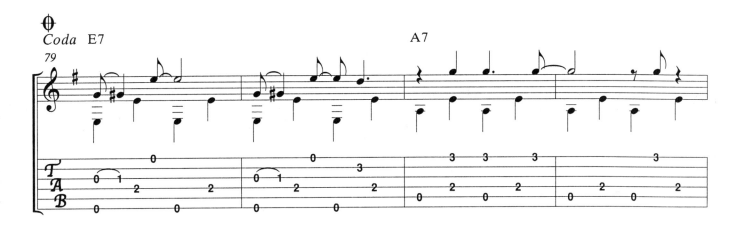

12

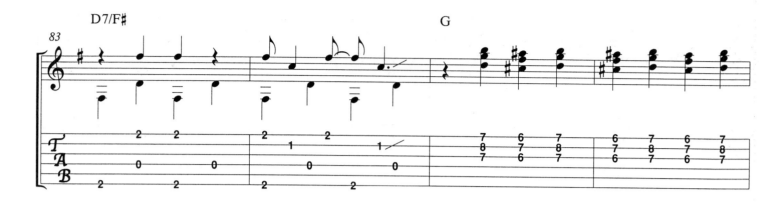

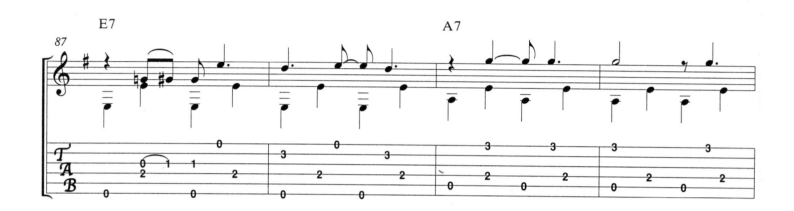

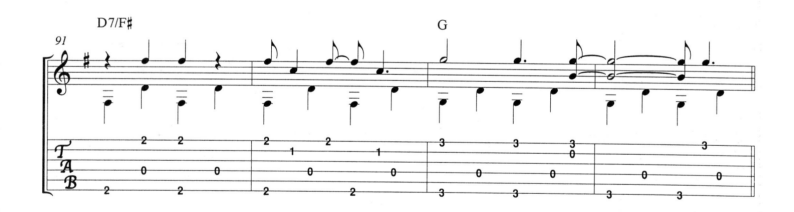

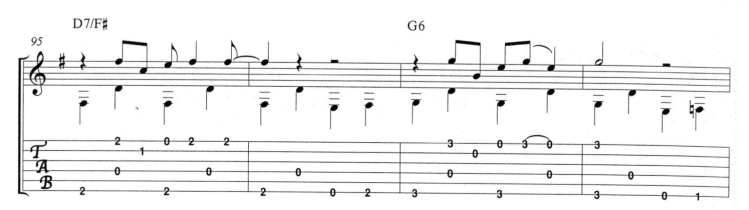

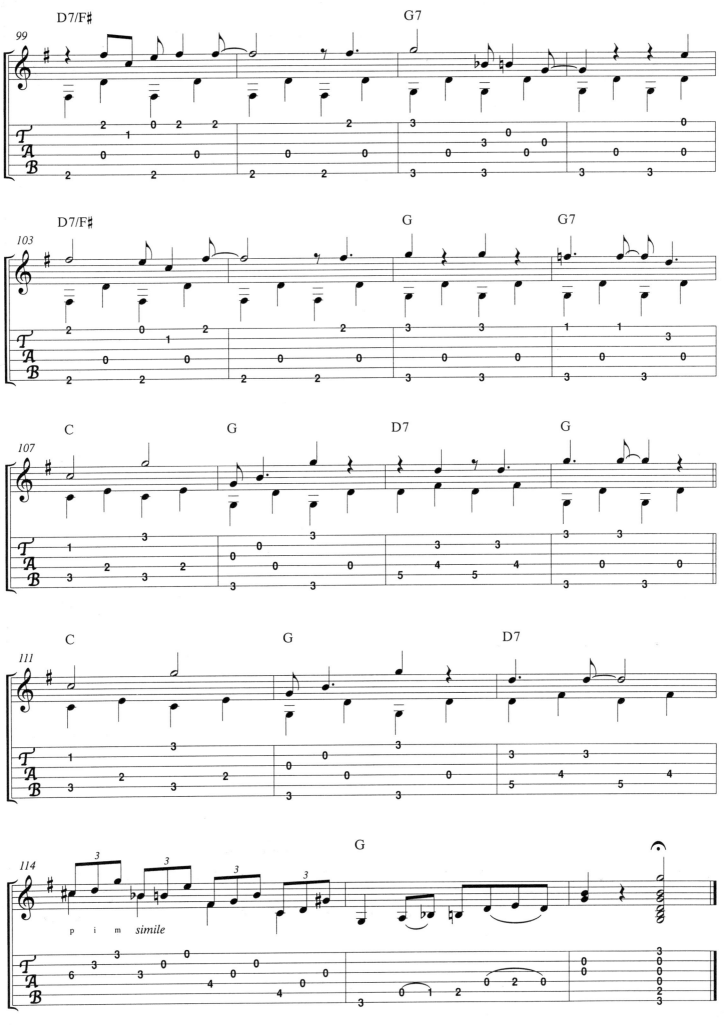

Funky Butt

By KENNY SULTAN

Moderately in 2 ♩ = 100

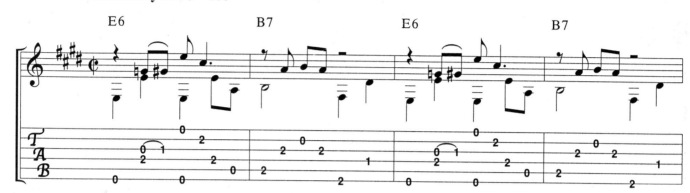

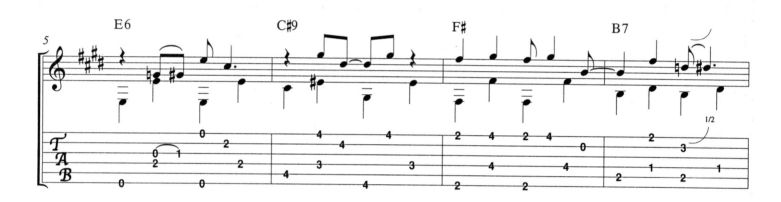

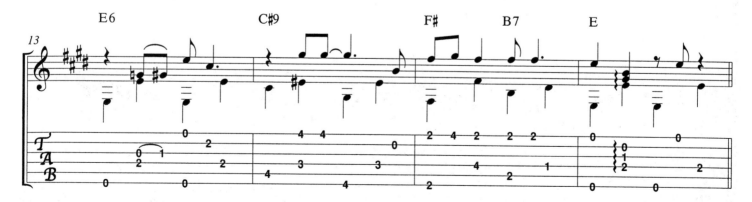

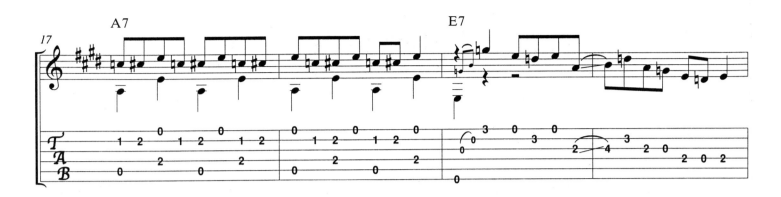

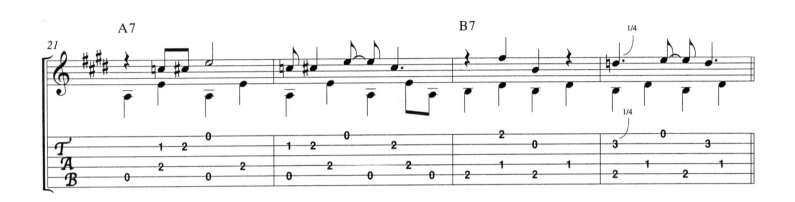

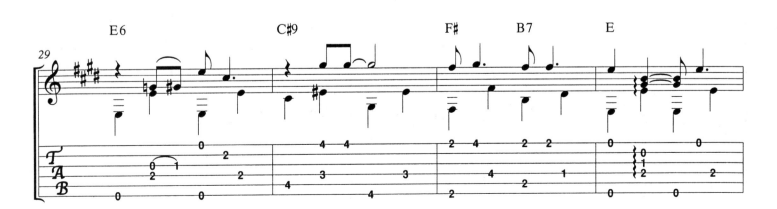

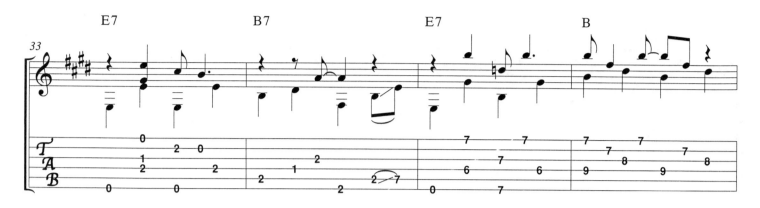

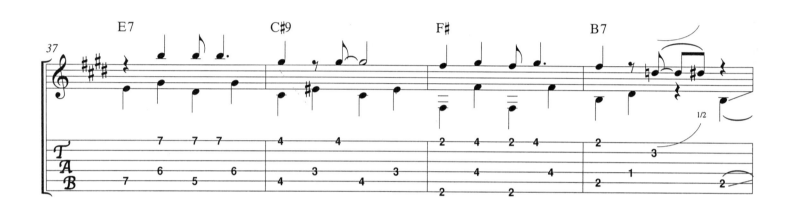

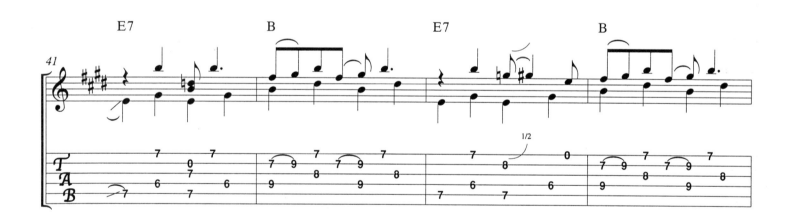

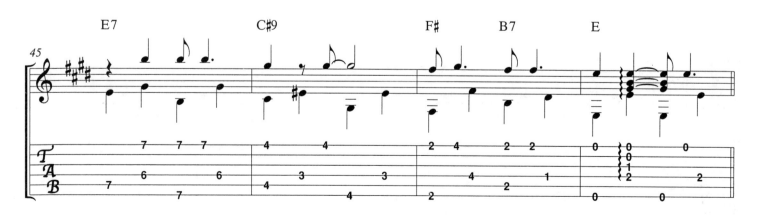

Honky Tonk

By KENNY SULTAN

Moderate shuffle ♩ = 125 (♫ = ♩³♪)

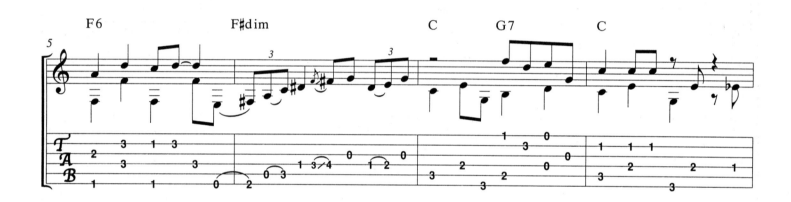

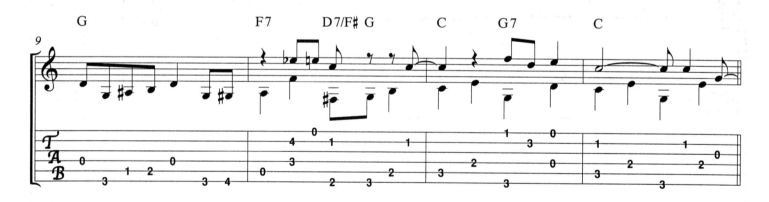

Honky Tonk - 6 - 1
SAIR006

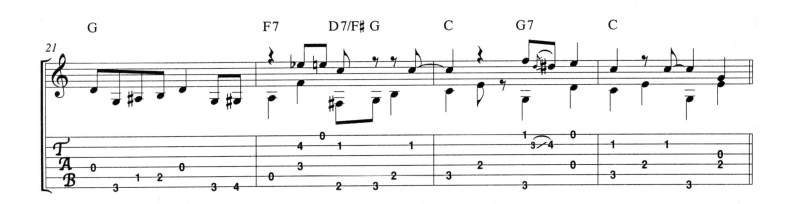

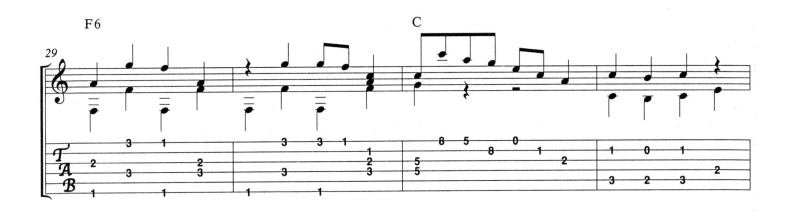

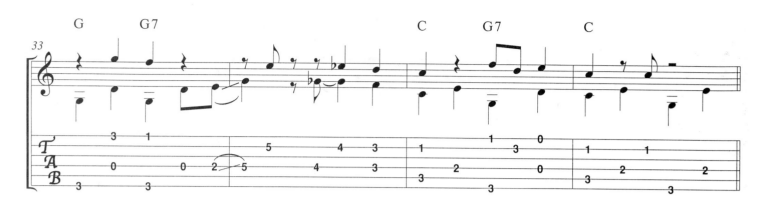

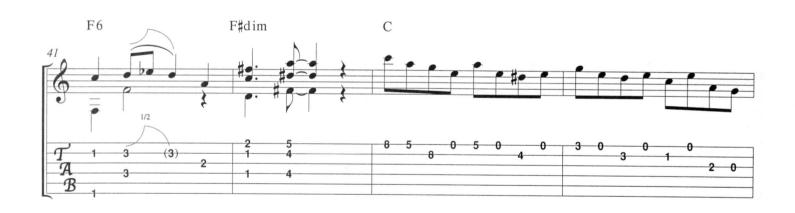

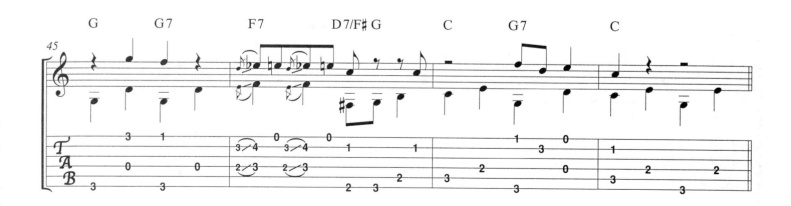

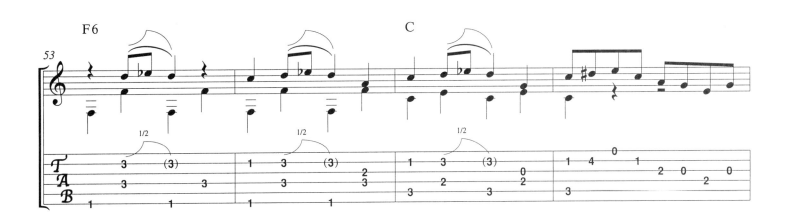

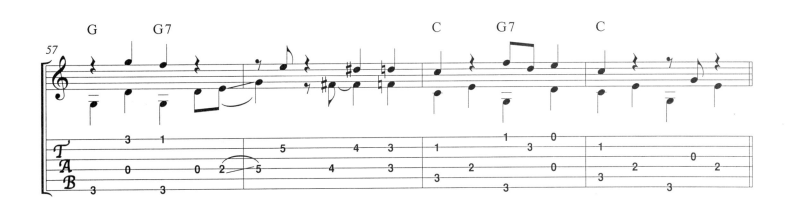

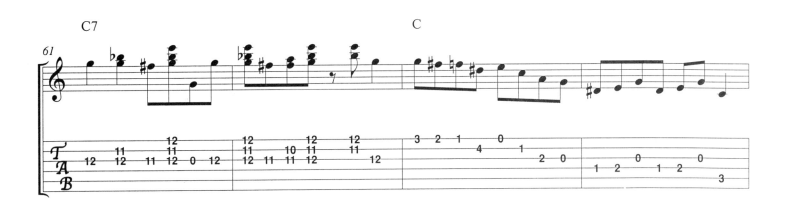

Honky Tonk - 6 - 4
SAIR006

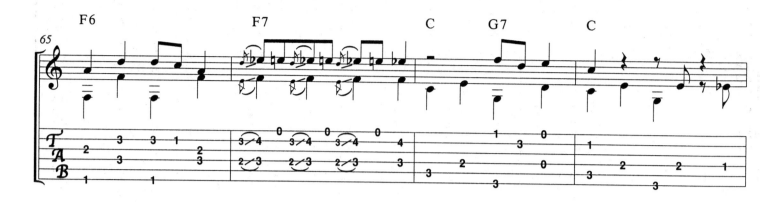

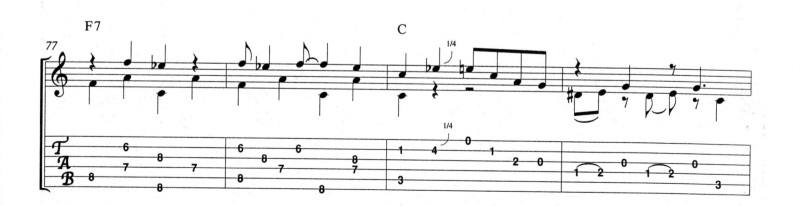

If The Shoe Fits

By KENNY SULTAN

Slow shuffle ♩ = 90 (♫ = ♪³♪)

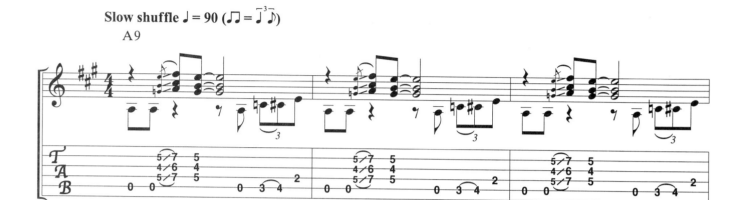

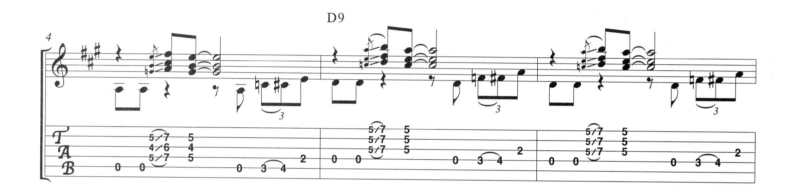

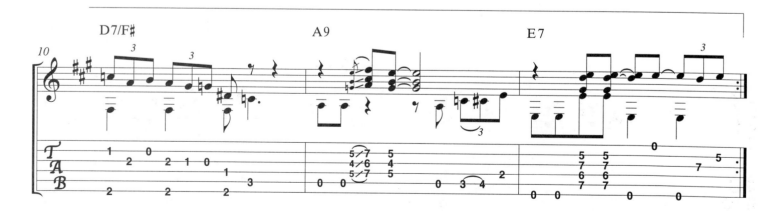

If the Shoe Fits - 5 - 1
SAIR006

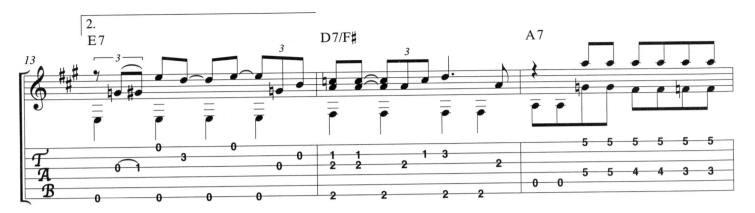

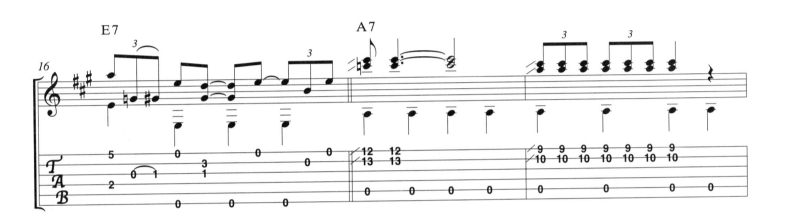

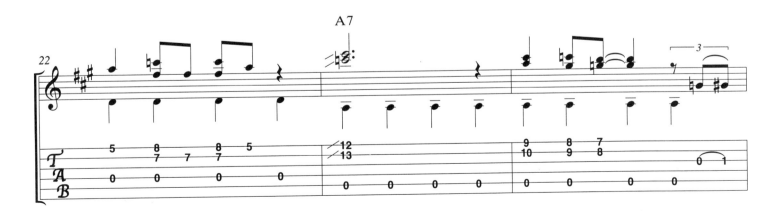

If the Shoe Fits - 5 - 2
SAIR006

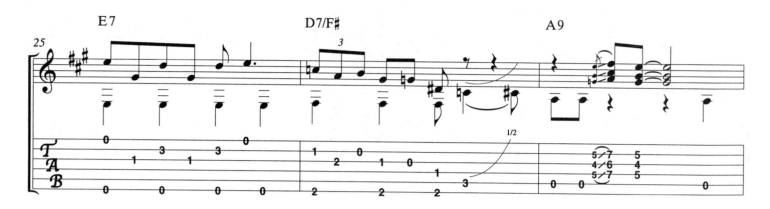

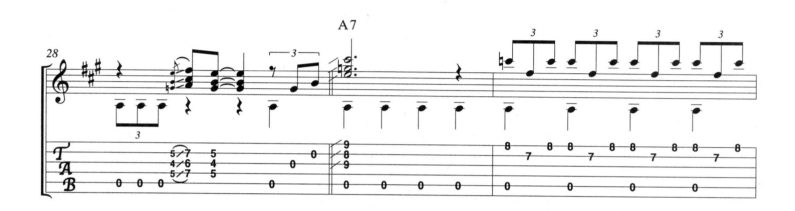

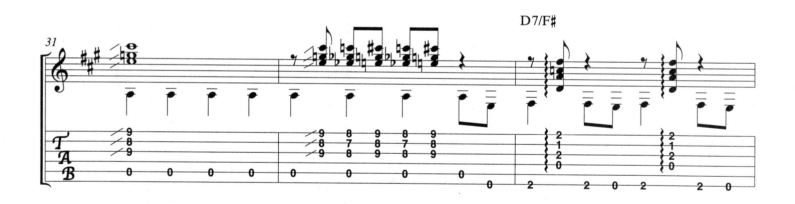

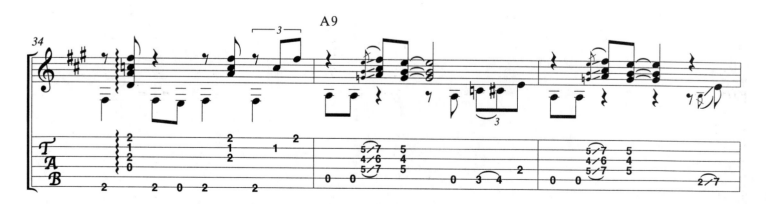

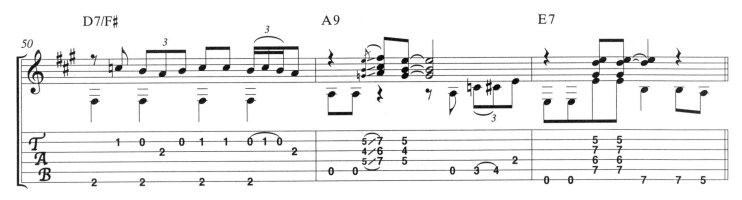

If the Shoe Fits - 5 - 4
SAIR006

28

If the Shoe Fits - 5 - 5
SAIR006

Lightnin' Strikes

By KENNY SULTAN

Medium fast shuffle ♩ = 130

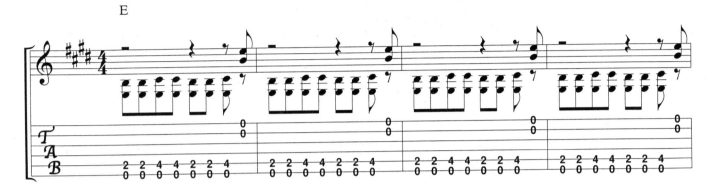

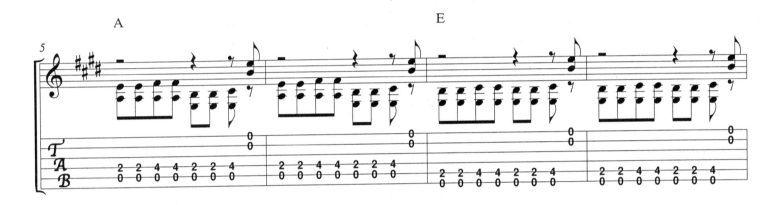

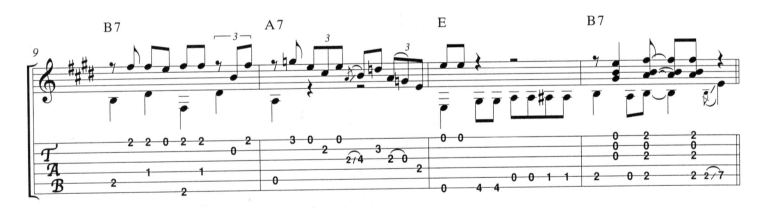

Lightnin' Strikes - 7 - 1
SAIR006

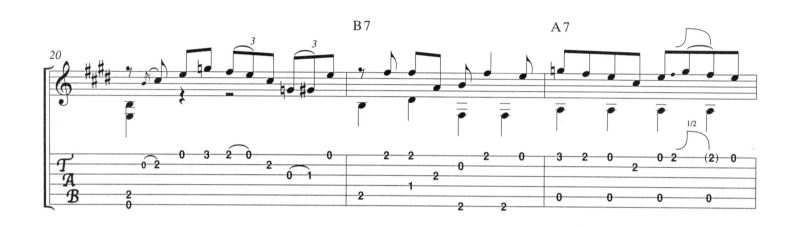

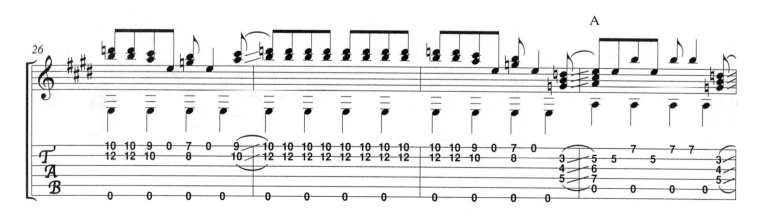

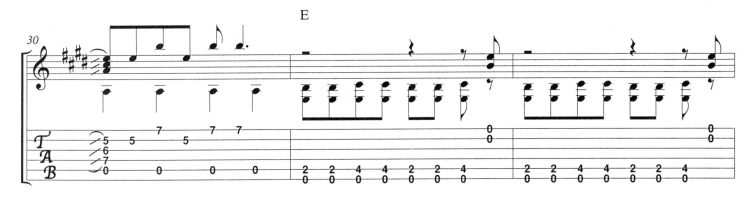

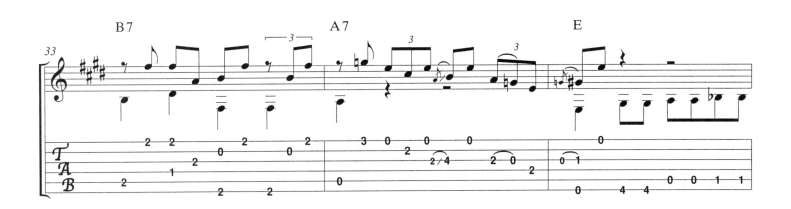

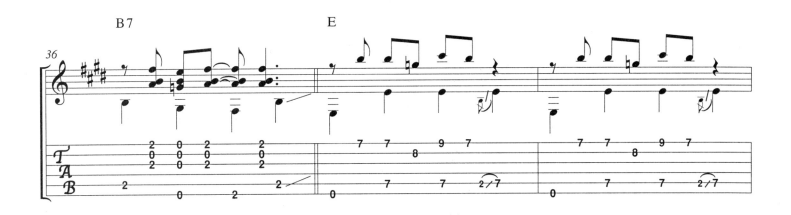

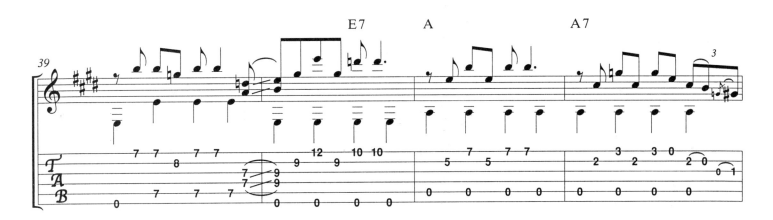

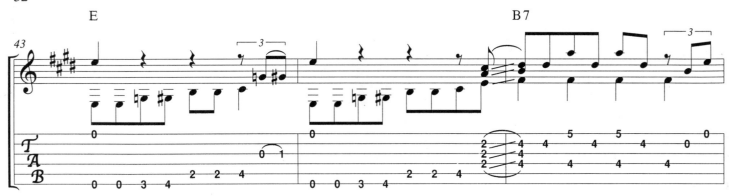

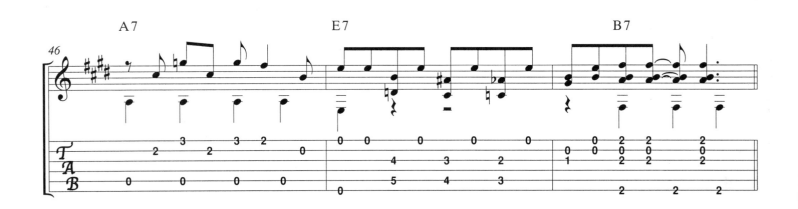

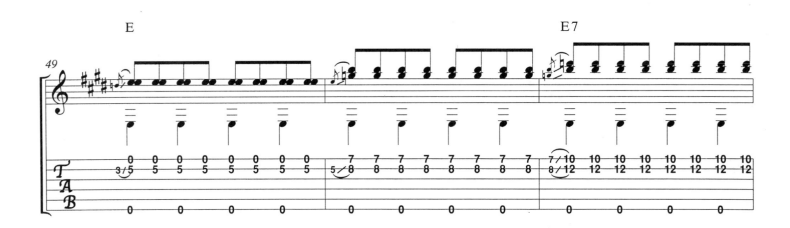

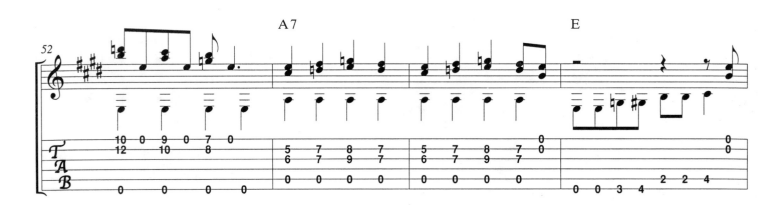

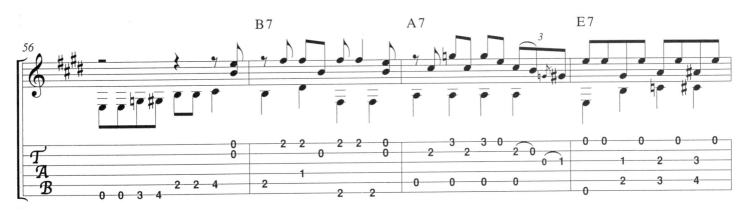

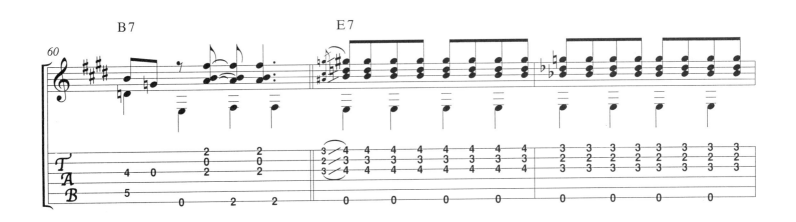

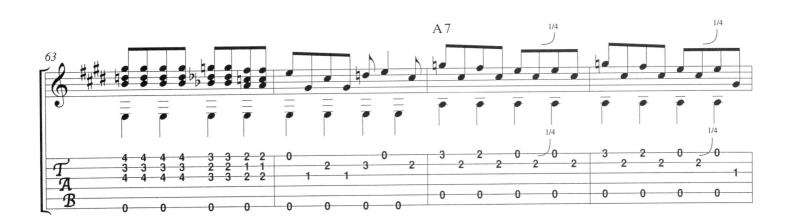

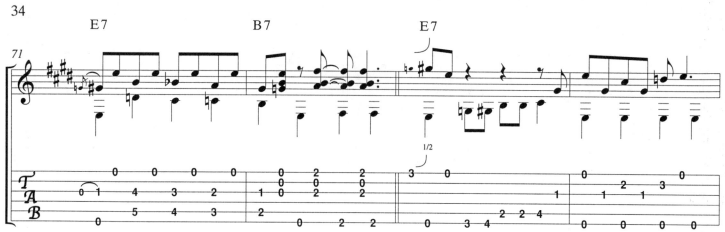

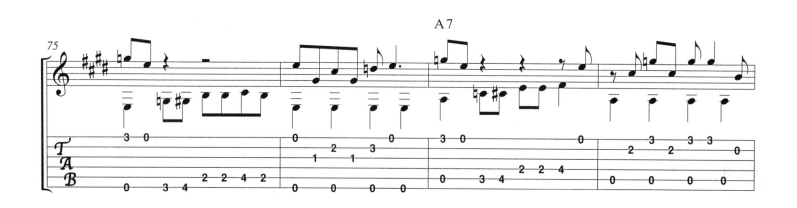

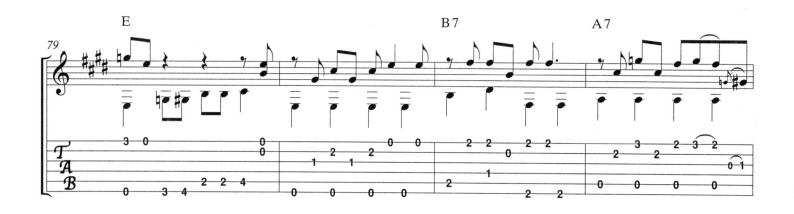

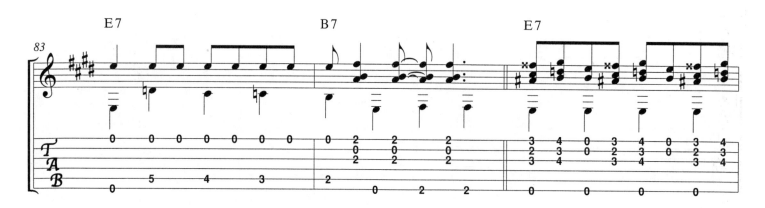

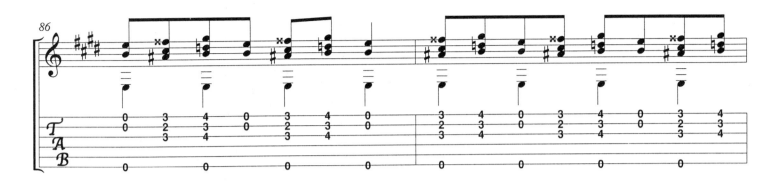

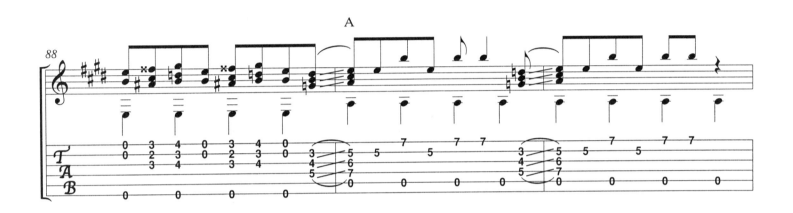

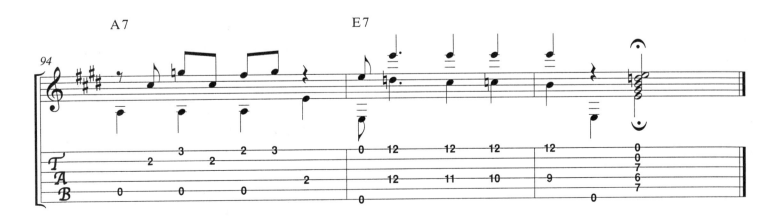

Read' Em And Weep

By KENNY SULTAN

Guitar tuned down 1/2 step:

⑥ = E♭ ③ = G♭
⑤ = A♭ ② = B♭
④ = D♭ ① = E♭

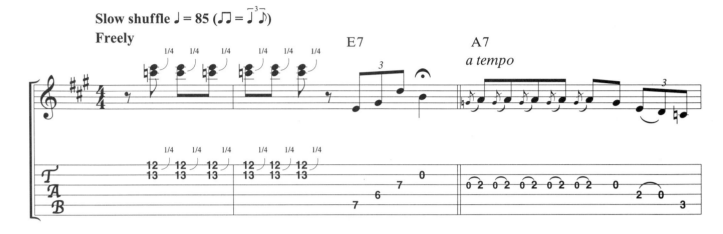

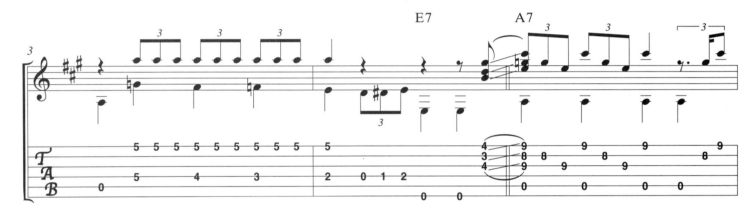

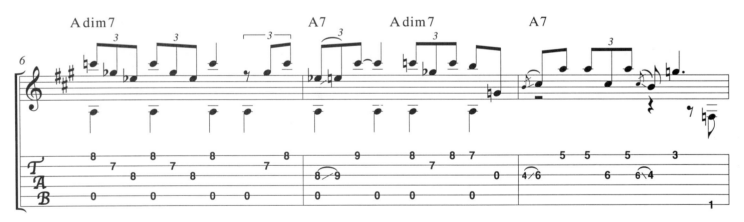

Read 'Em and Weep - 4 - 1
SAIR006

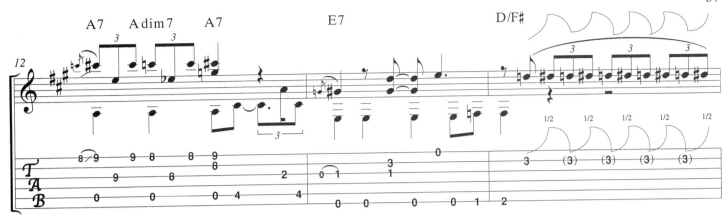

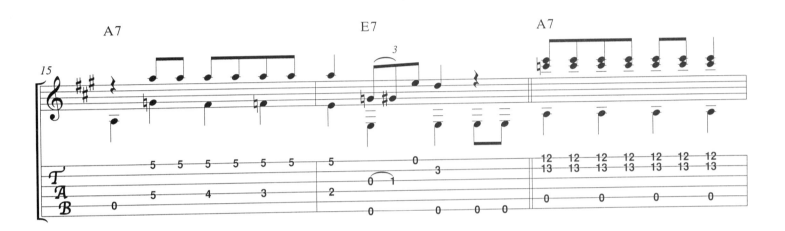

The Sick Boogie

By KENNY SULTAN

Moderately fast swing, in 2 ♩ = 120 (♫ = ♪³♪)

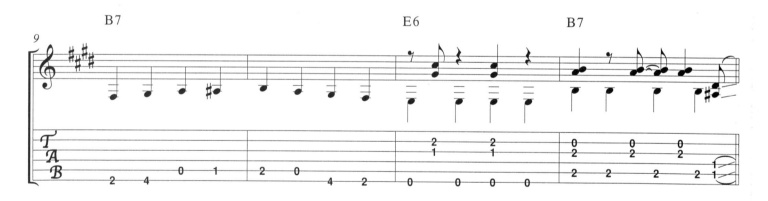

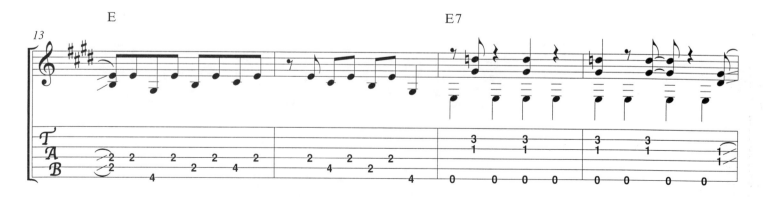

The Sick Boogie - 8 - 1
SAIR006

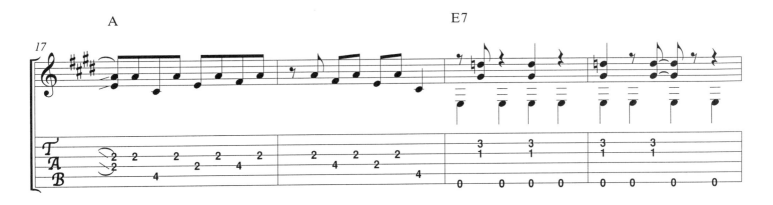

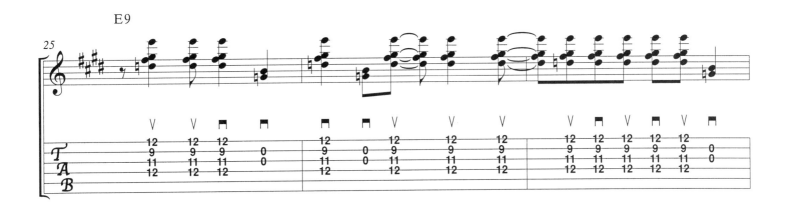

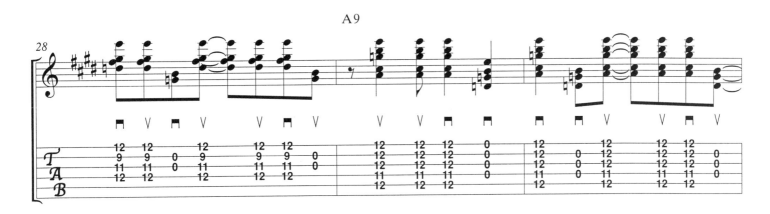

The Sick Boogie - 8 - 2
SAIR006

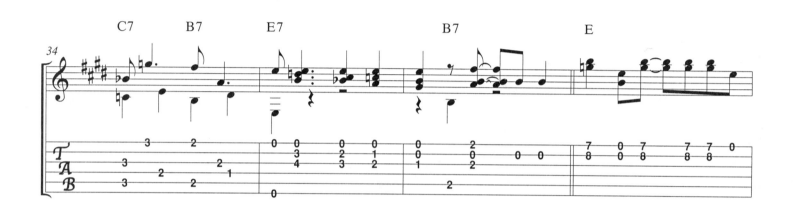

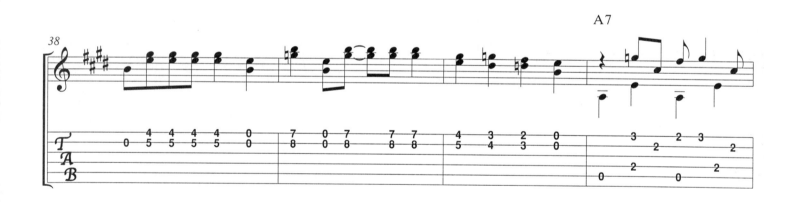

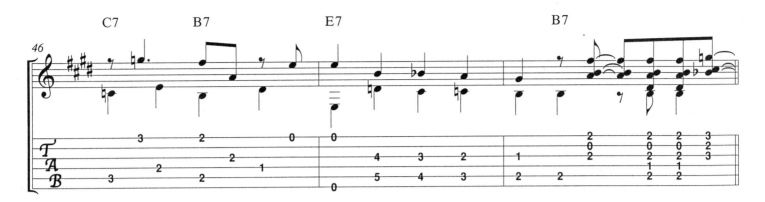

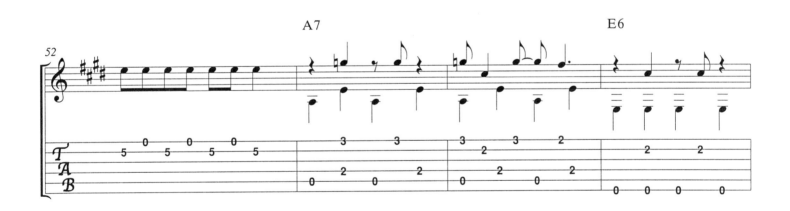

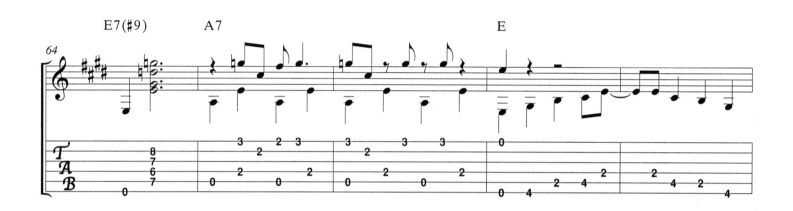

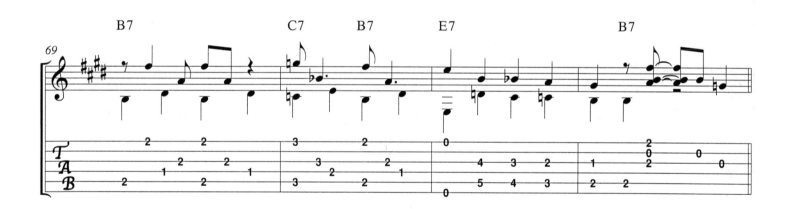

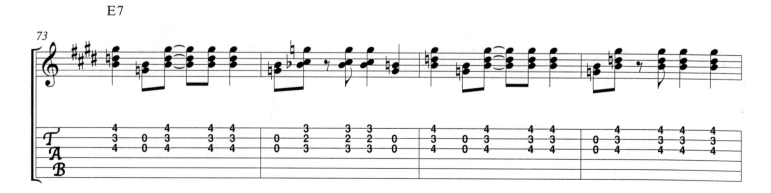

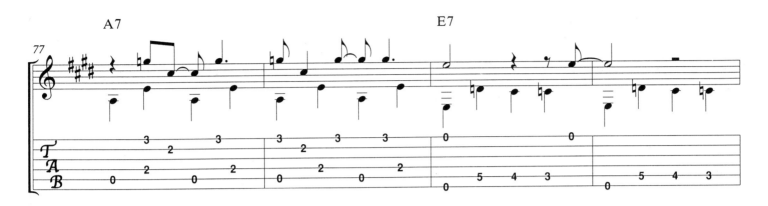

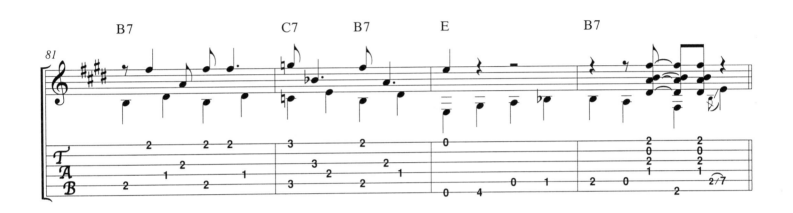

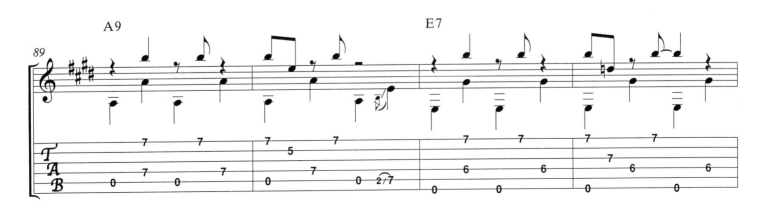

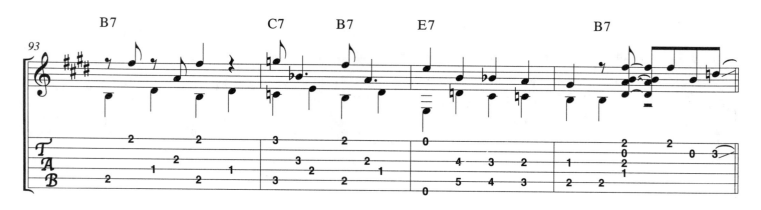

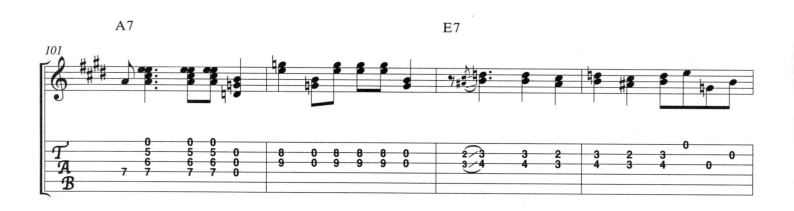

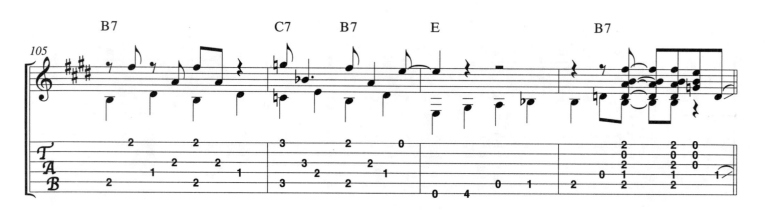

The Sick Boogie - 8 - 7

SAIR006

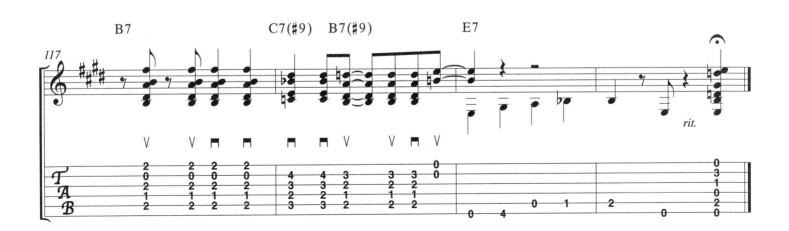

The Sick Boogie - 8 - 8
SAIR006

Slippin' and Drippin'

Guitar tuned down 1/2 step:

⑥ = E♭ ③ = G♭
⑤ = A♭ ② = B♭
④ = D♭ ① = E♭

By KENNY SULTAN

Slow shuffle ♩ = 82 (♫ = ♪³♪)
Freely
N.C.

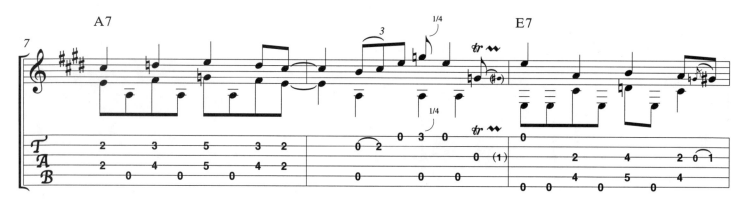

Slippin' and Drippin' - 7 - 1
SAIR006

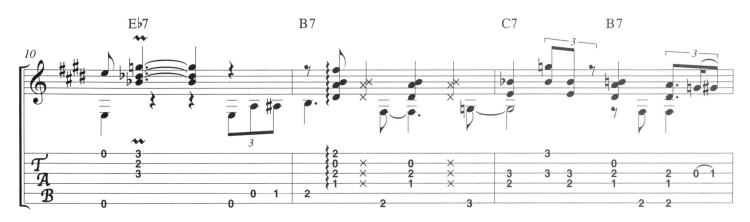

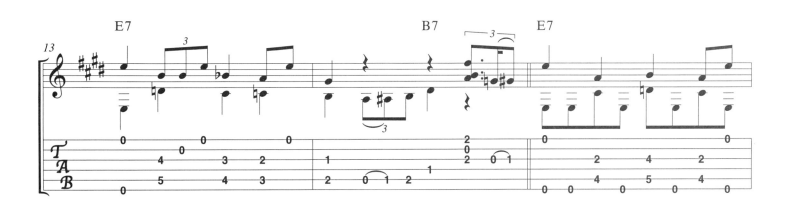

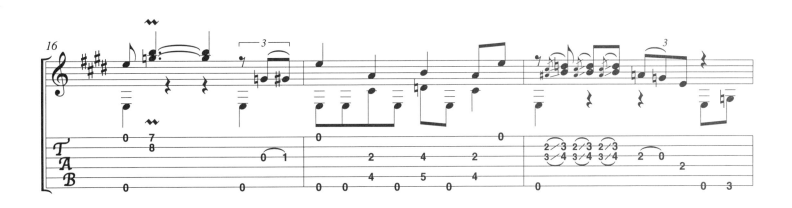

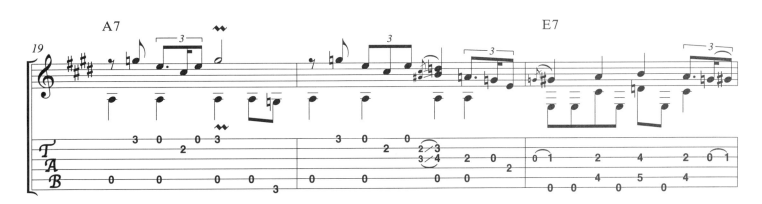

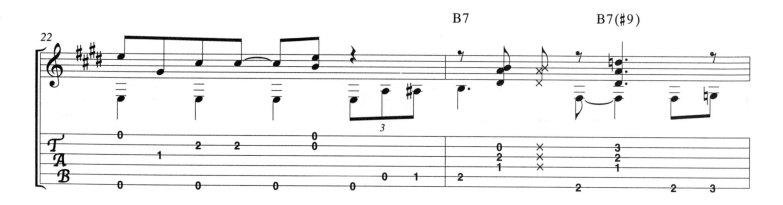

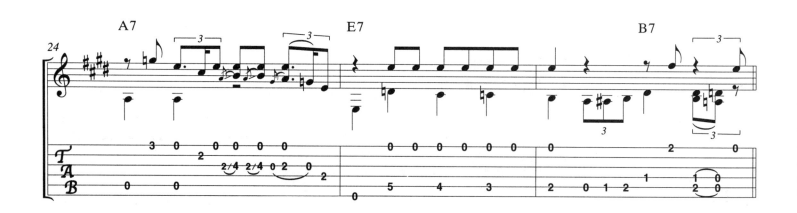

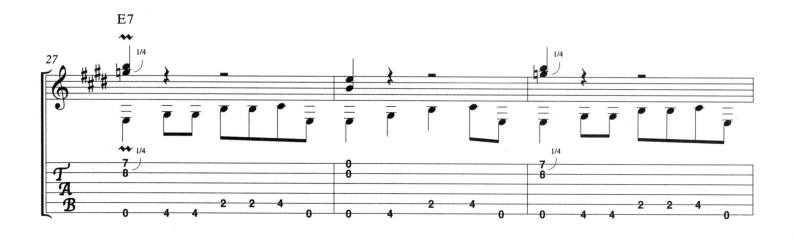

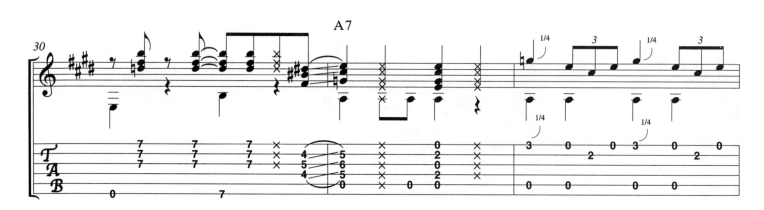

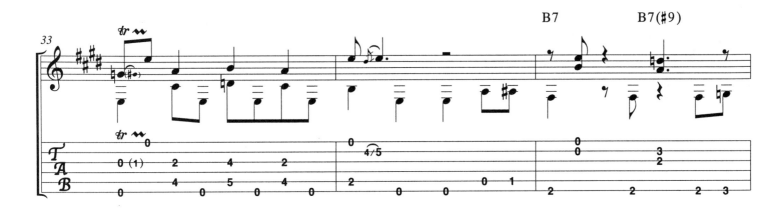

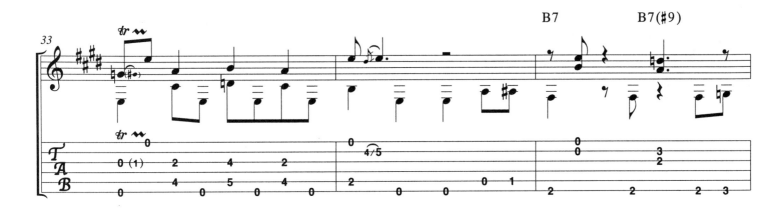

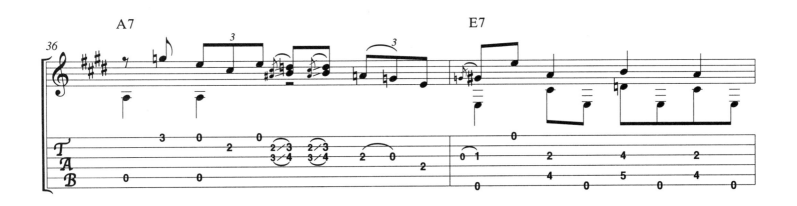

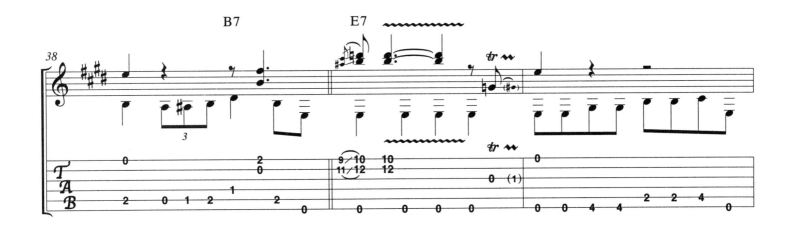

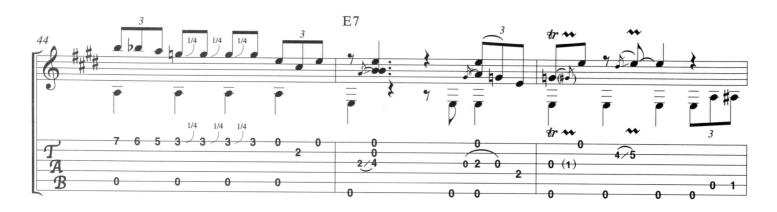

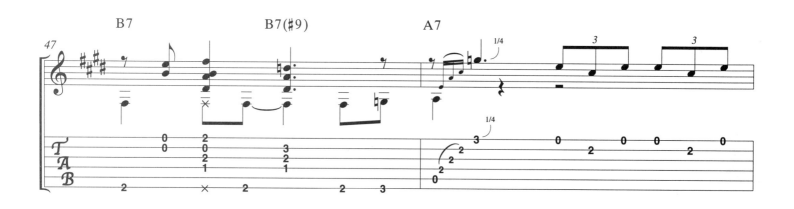

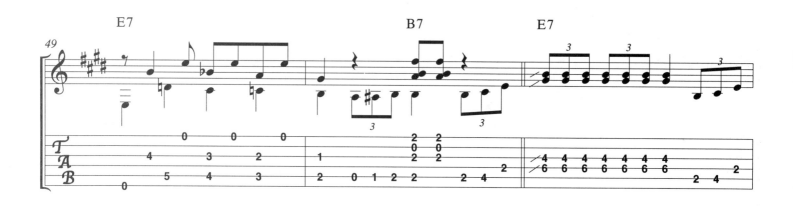

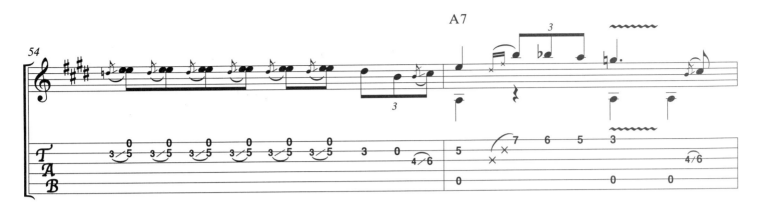

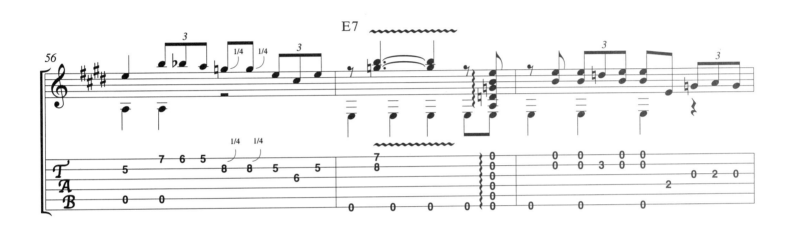

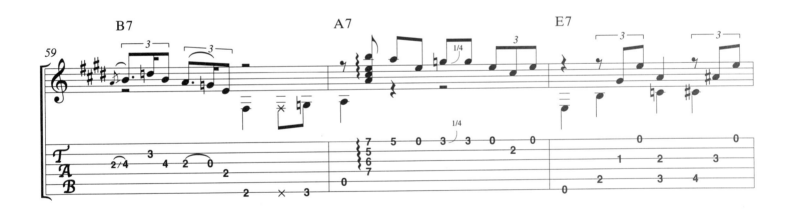

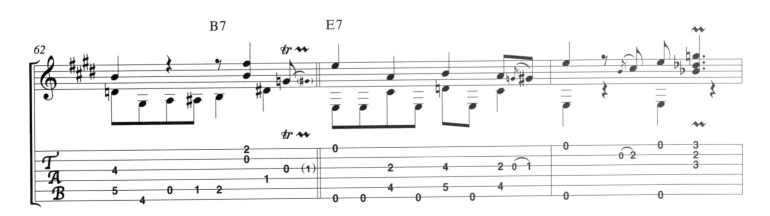

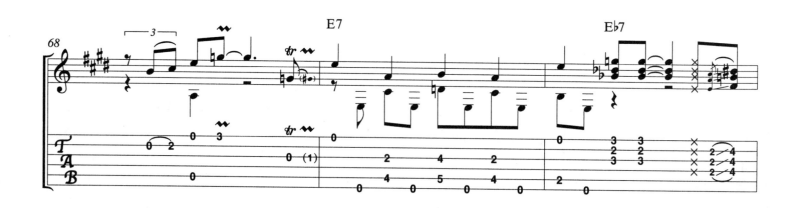

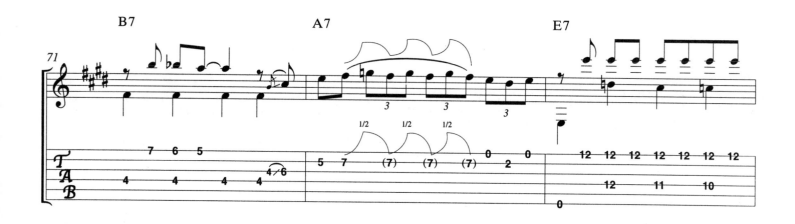

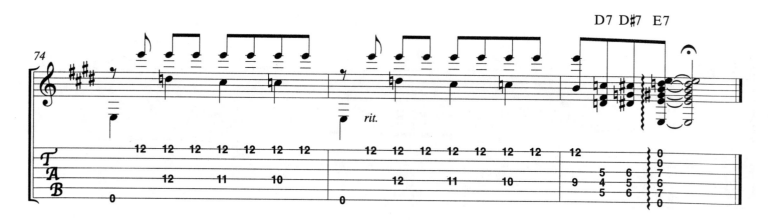

West Coast Blues

By KENNY SULTAN

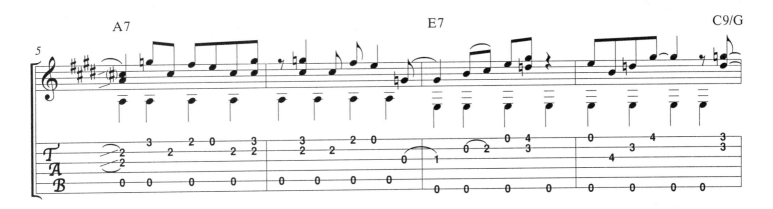

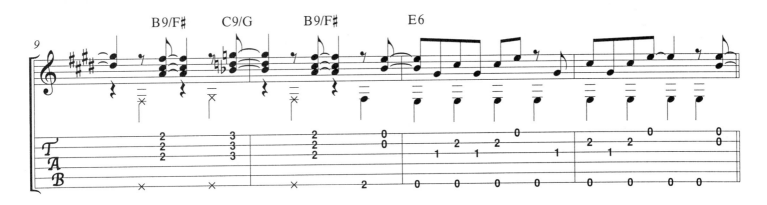

West Coast Blues - 5 - 1
SAIR006

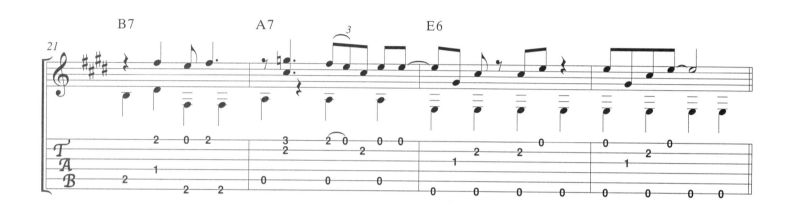

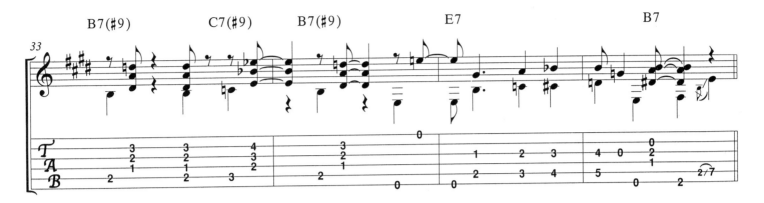

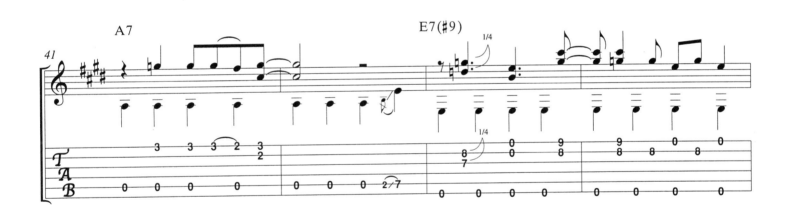

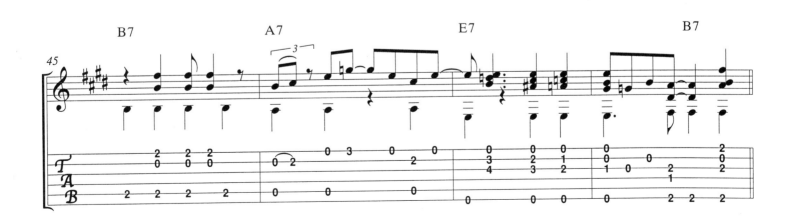

58

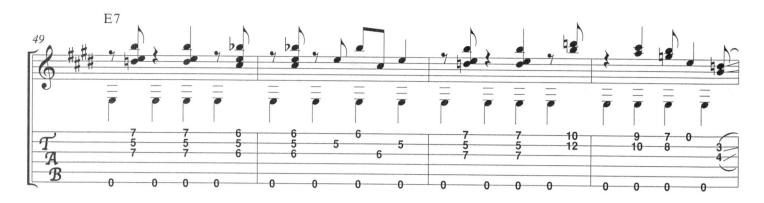

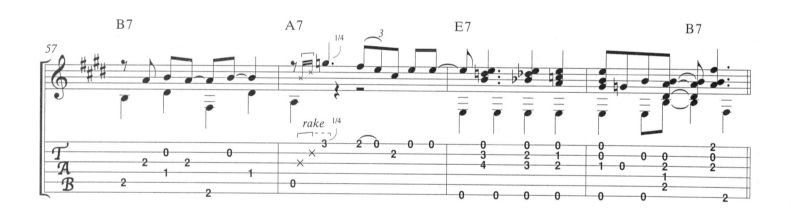

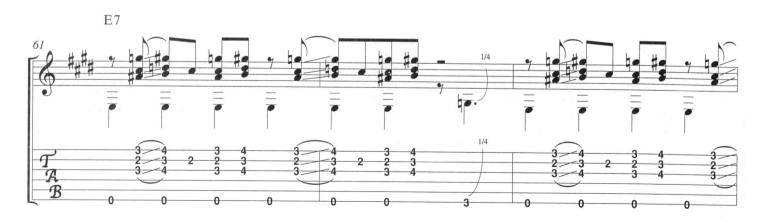

Suspicious Strut

Guitar capo 2

By KENNY SULTAN

Moderately fast ragtime, in 2 ♩ = 110

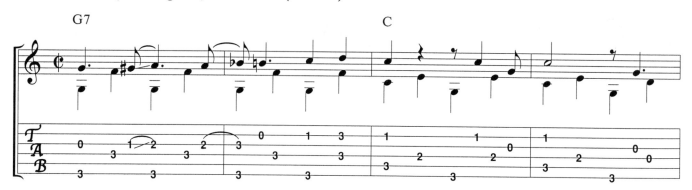

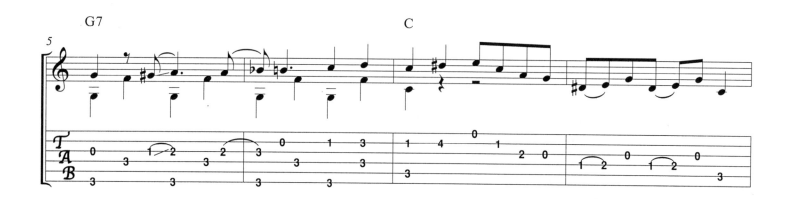

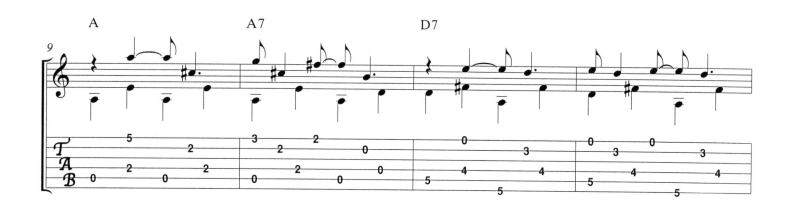

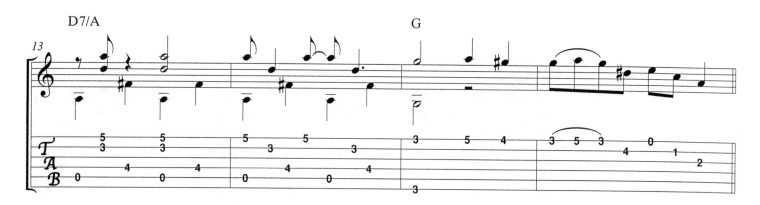

Suspicious Strut - 8 - 1
SAIR006

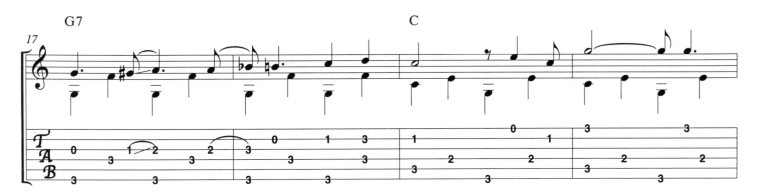

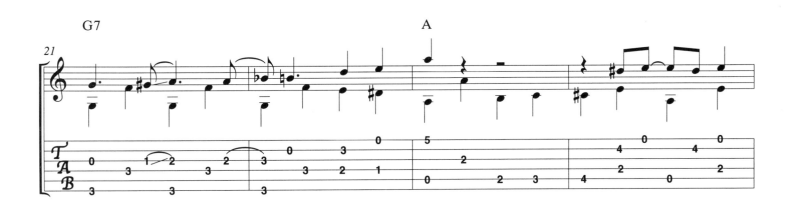

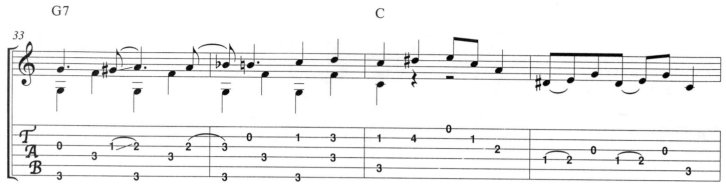

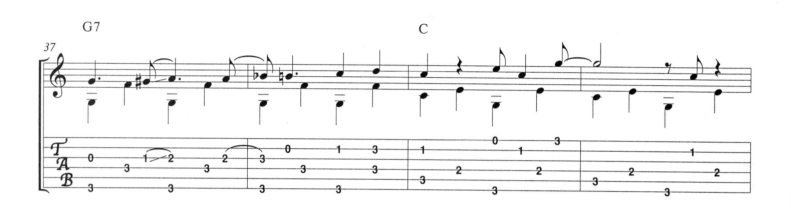

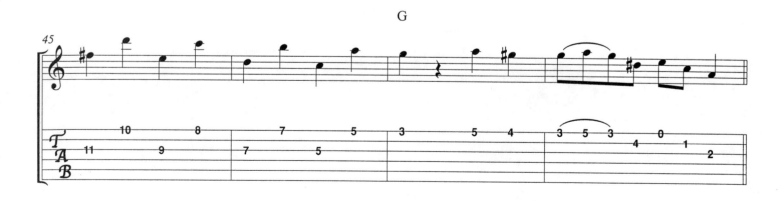

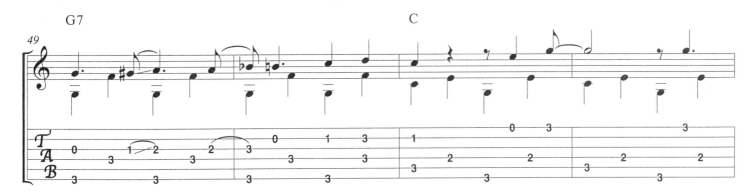

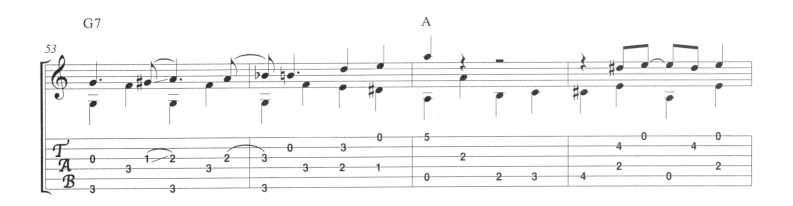

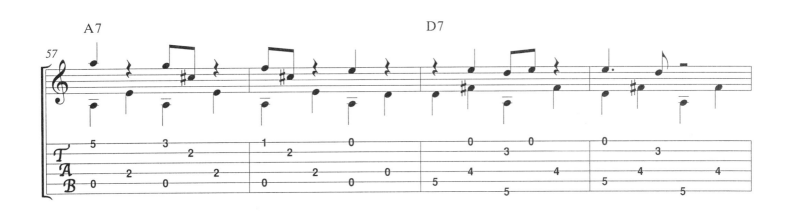

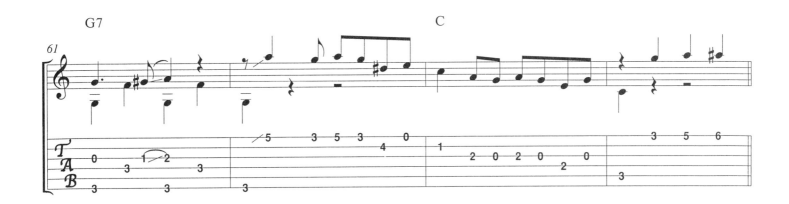

64

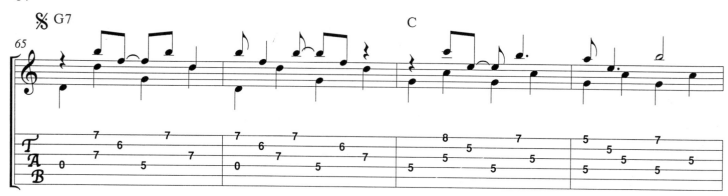

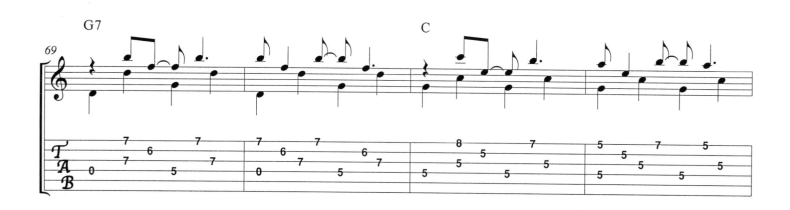

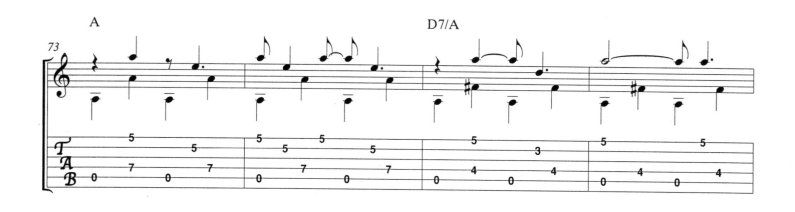

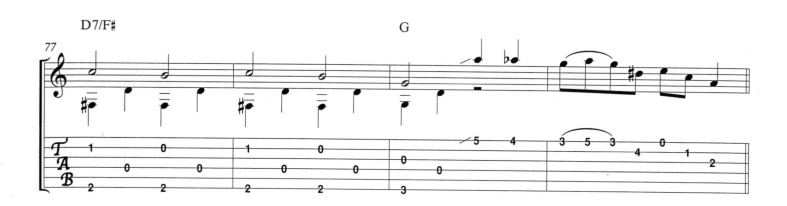

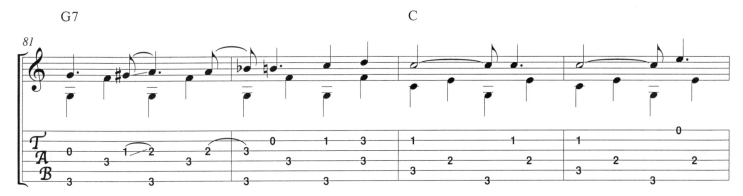

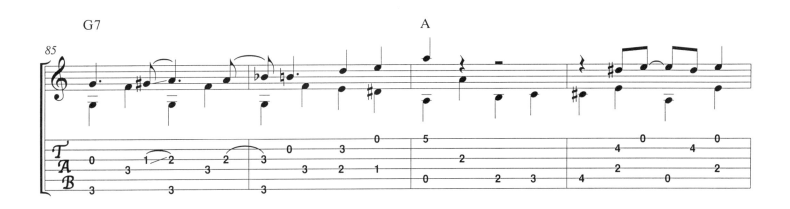

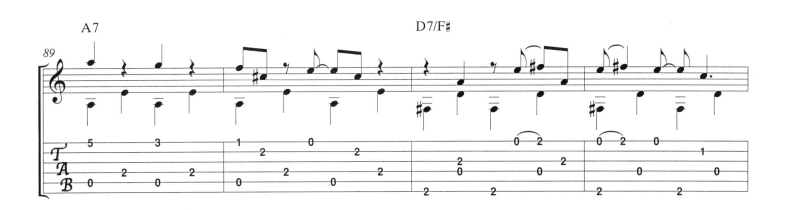

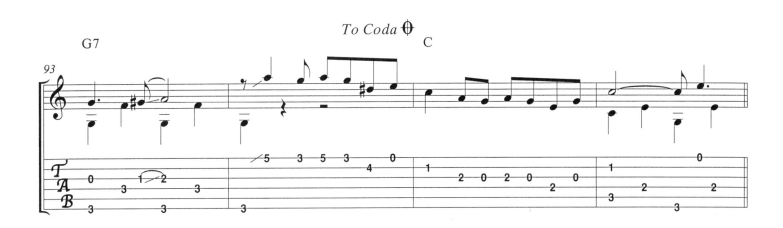

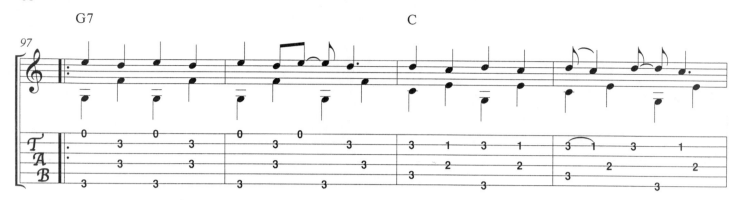

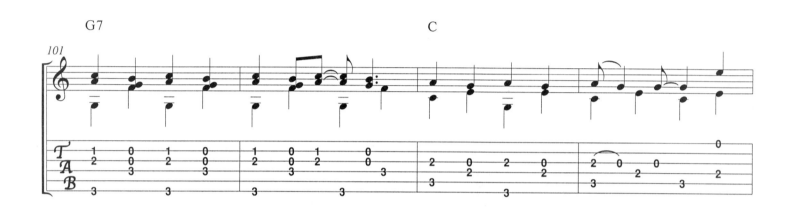

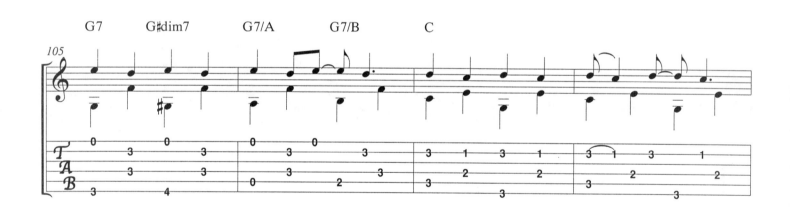

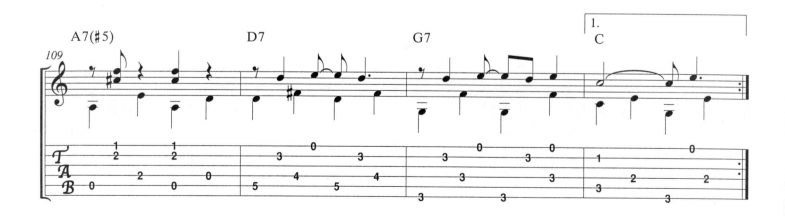

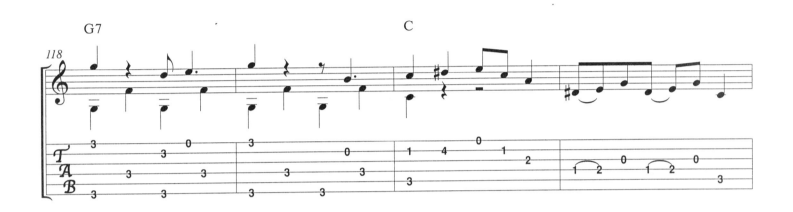

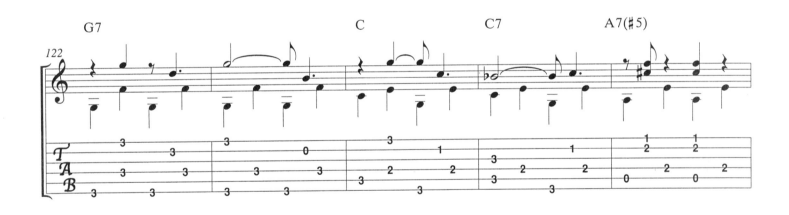

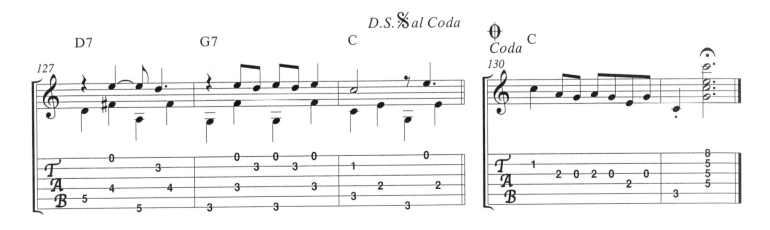

GUITAR TAB GLOSSARY **

TABLATURE EXPLANATION

READING TABLATURE: Tablature illustrates the six strings of the guitar. Notes and chords are indicated by the placement of fret numbers on a given string(s).

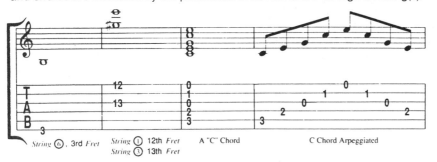

String ⑥, 3rd Fret   String ① 12th Fret   A "C" Chord   C Chord Arpeggiated
String ③ 13th Fret

BENDING NOTES

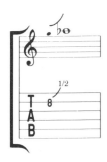

HALF STEP: Play the note and bend string one half step.*

PREBEND AND RELEASE: Bend the string, play it, then release to the original note.

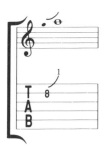

WHOLE STEP: Play the note and bend string one whole step.

RHYTHM SLASHES

STRUM INDICA- TIONS: Strum with indicated rhythm.

The chord voicings are found on the first page of the transcription underneath the song title.

INDICATING SINGLE NOTES USING RHYTHM SLASHES: Very often single notes are incorporated into a rhythm part. The note name is indicated above the rhythm slash with a fret number and a string indication.

*A half step is the smallest interval in Western music; it is equal to one fret. A whole step equals two frets.

**By Kenn Chipkin and Aaron Stang

ARTICULATIONS

HAMMER ON: Play lower note, then "hammer on" to higher note with another finger. Only the first note is attacked.

PULL OFF: Play higher note, then "pull off" to lower note with another finger. Only the first note is attacked.

LEGATO SLIDE: Play note and slide to the following note. (Only first note is attacked).

PALM MUTE: The note or notes are muted by the palm of the pick hand by lightly touching the string(s) near the bridge.

ACCENT: Notes or chords are to be played with added emphasis.

DOWN STROKES AND UPSTROKES: Notes or chords are to be played with either a downstroke (⊓ ·) or upstroke (∨) of the pick.

Kenny Sultan

Guitarist

Kenny began playing guitar when he was seven. Soon thereafter, his brother introduced him to the blues of T-Bone Walker and Lightnin' Hopkins. The effect was permanent. Confirming his love for music and the blues, he graduated with honors from the University of California at Santa Barbara, where he majored in music/ethnomusicology. A noted teacher, he has taught music, guitar, and music history at the university level and has conducted countless workshops and seminars. In addition to recording with Tom Ball, Kenny has appeared as a sideman on numerous recordings by other artists and has two widely acclaimed solo guitar CDs on Solid Air Records.

In 2001, Kenny released his first solo CD, *West Coast Blues.* At the suggestion of executive producer James Jensen to "keep it funky and play from the heart," Kenny states, "This music is played as if I were sitting on my couch around midnight playing for myself." *Acoustic Guitar* magazine described it as "fluid grooves and a slew of very tasty licks." *West Coast Blues* was so well received that Kenny followed it up with *Guitar Blues,* also on Solid Air Records.

Kenny's most recent solo project has been the newly released multi-angle instructional/concert DVD *Kenny Sultan: Guitar Blues* (Solid Air Records, distributed by Warner Bros. Publications). It has been called "a virtual encyclopedia of blues licks and patterns!"

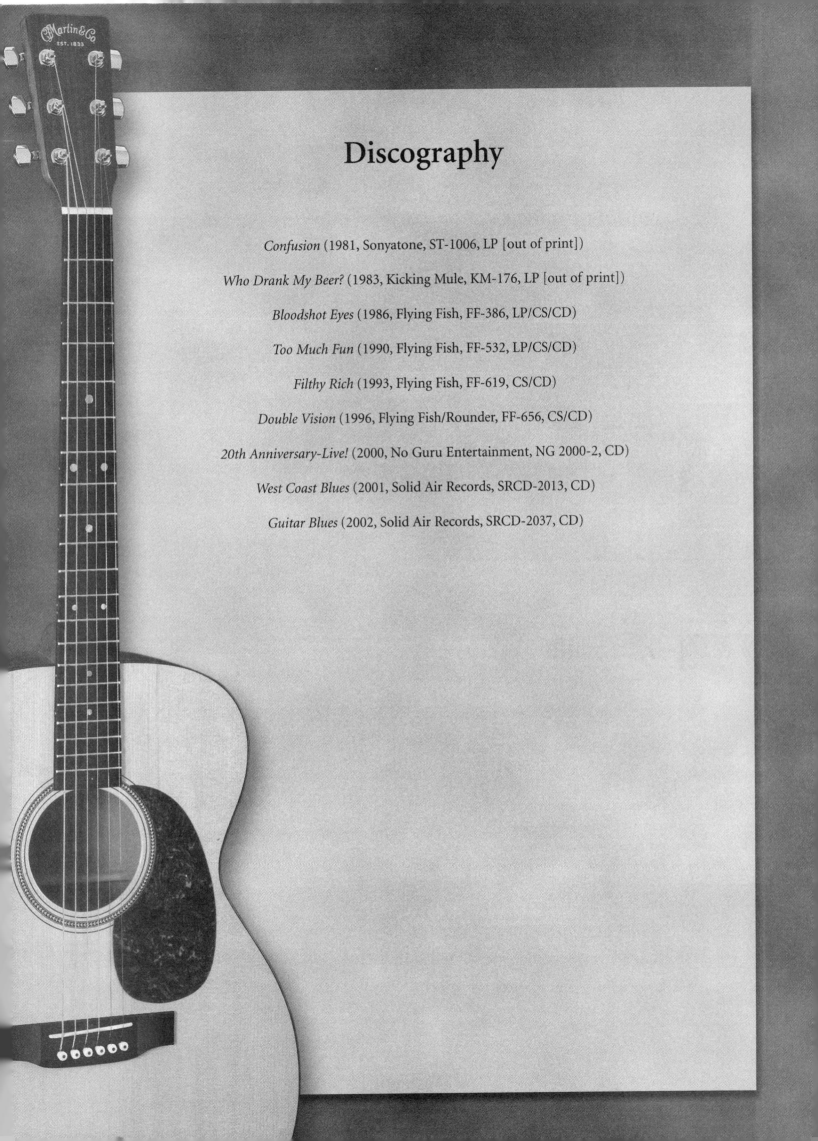

Discography

Confusion (1981, Sonyatone, ST-1006, LP [out of print])

Who Drank My Beer? (1983, Kicking Mule, KM-176, LP [out of print])

Bloodshot Eyes (1986, Flying Fish, FF-386, LP/CS/CD)

Too Much Fun (1990, Flying Fish, FF-532, LP/CS/CD)

Filthy Rich (1993, Flying Fish, FF-619, CS/CD)

Double Vision (1996, Flying Fish/Rounder, FF-656, CS/CD)

20th Anniversary-Live! (2000, No Guru Entertainment, NG 2000-2, CD)

West Coast Blues (2001, Solid Air Records, SRCD-2013, CD)

Guitar Blues (2002, Solid Air Records, SRCD-2037, CD)

Solid Air Records Presents
The Finest Acoustic Guitarists on DVD

Laurence Juber
The Guitarist
906729

The premier solo acoustic guitarist of our generation performs and explains six of his most popular solo guitar pieces in DADGAD and standard tuning.

Mike Dowling
Uptown Blues
906841

Mike Dowling performs a unique blend of blues, ragtime, swing, and roots music in standard and open tunings.

David Cullen
Jazz, Classical and Beyond
906843

David Cullen's influences, which range from gospel to jazz and funk to classical music, combine to give him a unique voice and a deep sense of composition.

Al Petteway
Celtic, Blues and Beyond
906844

Al Petteway's compositions incorporate Celtic, blues, and R&B influences. Al also offers some great tips on how to color compositions with techniques that make the music sing.

Doug Smith
Contemporary Instrumental Guitar
906842

With a background in classical guitar and composition and a rock band honored by *Musician* magazine as the finest in the country, Doug Smith brings these diverse influences to his contemporary instrumentals.

Kenny Sultan
Guitar Blues
906840

Kenny Sultan teaches six of his own compositions. These pieces serve as a virtual encyclopedia of blues licks and patterns.

Also Available as Books/CDs

Each book contains note-for-note guitar arrangements transcribed by the artists themselves in standard notation and tab. Plus, you get a masterclass-style CD on which the artist walks you carefully through the key aspects and techniques for each arrangement.

Laurence Juber:
The Guitarist Anthology, Vol. 1 (SAIR001)
The Guitarist Anthology, Vol. 2 (SAIR002)

David Cullen:
Grateful Guitar (SAIR003)
Jazz, Classical and Beyond (SAIR004)

Doug Smith:
Contemporary Instrumental Guitar (SAIR005)

Kenny Sultan:
Guitar Blues (SAIR006)

Mike Dowling:
Uptown Blues (SAIR007)

Al Petteway:
Celtic, Blues and Beyond (SAIR008)

AD1135 11/03